ABBA®

GOLD

GREATEST HITS

Dancing Queen

Words & Music by Benny Andersson, Stig Anderson & Bjorn Ulvaeus.

danc - ing__ queen.

Fri-day night and the lights are low,__

look-ing out__ for a place to go,__ Oh,__ where they play the right mu-sic,

get-ting in__ the swing, you come to look for a king.__

7

8

9

Take A Chance On Me

Words & Music by Benny Andersson & Bjorn Ulvaeus.

take a chance on me,___ gon-na do my ve - ry best and it ain't no lie,___

if you put me to___ the test, if you let me try,___ take a

chance on me,_____ take a chance on me._____

Oh you can take your time ba - by,___ I'm in no___ hur - ry,___ I

We can go___ dan - cing, we can go___ walk - ing,___ as

12

to go when you're feel-ing down.___ If you're all a - lone___

when the pret - ty birds___ have flown, ho-ney I'm still free,___ take a chance on me,___

gon-na do my ve - ry best ba-by, can't you see___ got-ta put me to___

the test, take a chance on me.___ If you change your mind

repeat and fade

15

Knowing Me, Knowing You

Words & Music by Benny Andersson, Stig Anderson & Bjorn Ulvaeus.

we're through. Break-in' up is ne-ver ea-sy I know, but I have to go. Know-ing me, know-ing you, it's the best_____ I can do.

18

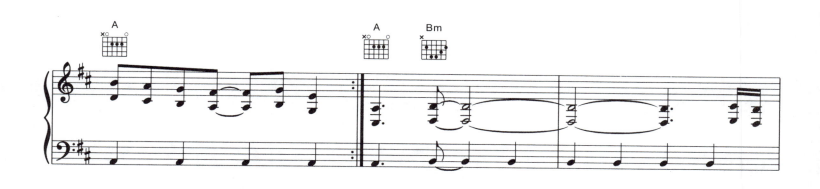

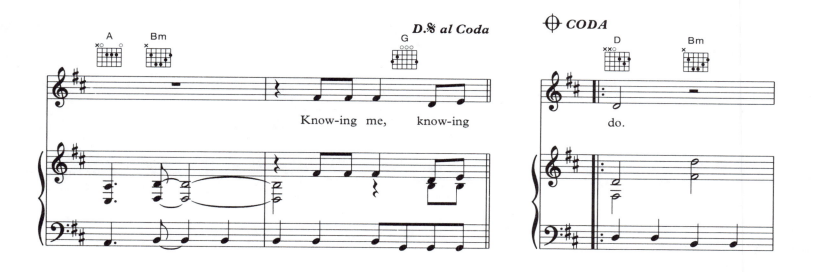

D.𝄋 al Coda

⊕ CODA

Know-ing me, know-ing

do.

repeat and fade

Mamma Mia

Words & Music by Benny Andersson, Stig Anderson & Bjorn Ulvaeus.

I've been cheat-ed by you____ since I don't__ know when,____

I've been an-gry and sad____ a-bout things that you do,____

so I made up my mind____ it must come to an end,____

I can't count all the times____ that I've told you we're through,

21

Super Trouper

Words & Music by Benny Andersson & Bjorn Ulvaeus.

So i-ma-gine I was glad to hear you're com-ing, sud-den-ly I feel al-right,
There are mo-ments when I think I'm go-ing cra-zy, but it's gon-na be al-right,

and it's gon-na be so dif-ferent when I'm on the stage to - night. _____ To-night the
ev - ery-thing will be so dif-ferent when I'm on the stage to - night. _____ To-night the

Su - per Trou - per lights are gon - na find me, shin - ing like the
Su - per. Trou - per lights are gon - na find me, shin - ing like the

sun, smil - ing, hav - ing fun,
sun, smil - ing, hav - ing fun,

feel-ing like a num-ber one. To-night the Su - per Trou - per
feel-ing like a num-ber one. To-night the Su - per Trou - per

beams are gon-na blind me but I won't feel blue
beams are gon-na blind me but I won't feel blue

like I al-ways do, 'cause some-where in the crowd there's
like I al-ways do, 'cause

some-where in the crowd there's you. So I'll be

there when you ar-rive, the sight of you will prove to me I'm still a-

-live and when you take me in your arms and hold me tight I

know it's gon-na mean so much to-night. _____ To-night the

D.S. and fade out

29

Lay All Your Love On Me

Words & Music by Benny Andersson & Bjorn Ulvaeus.

I was-n't jeal-ous be-fore we met,
now ev-'ry wo-man I see is a po-

It was like shoot-ing a sit-ting duck,
a lit-tle small-talk, a smile and, ba-by,

I've had a few lit-tle love af-fairs,
they did-n't last ver-y long and they've been

- ten-tial threat,
I was stuck.
pret-ty scarce.

and I'm po - sess - sive, it is - n't nice,
I still don't know what you've done with me,
I used to think   that was sen- si - ble,

you've heard me say - ing that smok - ing   was   my   on - ly vice.
a grown-up wo - man should nev - er   fall   so   eas - i - ly.
it makes the truth   ev - en more   in - comp - re - hen-si - ble.

But
I
'Cause

now it is - n't true,
feel a kind   of fear
ev - 'ry-thing is new,

now ev - 'ry-thing is new
when I don't have you near,
and ev - 'ry-thing is you,

and
un -
and

31

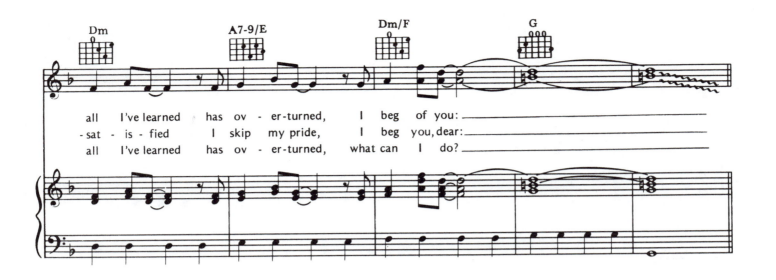

all I've learned has ov-er-turned, I beg of you: _____
-sat-is-fied I skip my pride, I beg you, dear: _____
all I've learned has ov-er-turned, what can I do? _____

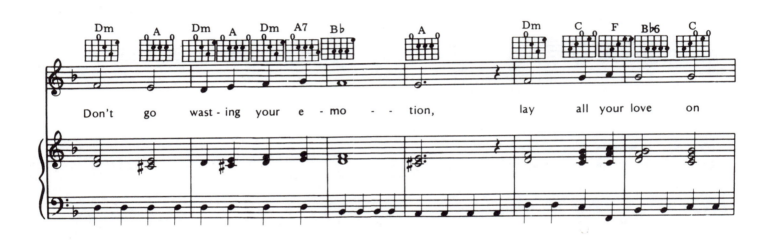

Don't go wast-ing your e-mo-tion, lay all your love on

me. _____

2.
Don't go shar-ing your de-vo - - tion, lay all your love on

me. _____

3.
Don't go shar-ing your de-
Don't go wast-ing your e-

-vo - - tion, lay all your love on me. _____
-mo - - tion,

Repeat and fade

I Have A Dream

Words & Music by Benny Andersson & Bjorn Ulvaeus.

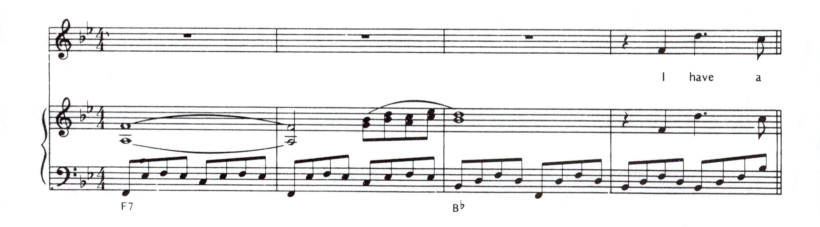

cope   with an - y - thing.   If you see the

F7   Bb

won - der   of a fair - y tale,   you can take the

F7   Bb

to Coda

fu - ture   ev - en if you fail.   I be - lieve in

F7   Bb

an - gels,   some-thing good in ev - ery-thing I see,   I be - lieve in

F7   Eb   Bb

an - gels

when I know the time is right for me. I'll cross the

F7   Eᵇ   Bᵇ

stream,

I have a dream.

I have a

F7   Bᵇ

dream,

a fan - ta - sy,

to help me

F7   Bᵇ

through _____ re - al - i - ty.

And my des - ti -

F7   Bᵇ

-na - tion   makes it worth the while   push-ing through the

F7   B♭

dark - ness   still an - oth - er mile.   I be - lieve _____

F7   B♭

_____ in an - gels,   some-thing good in ev - ery-thing I

F7   E♭

see,   I be - lieve in an - gels   when I know the

B♭   F7

time is right for me. I'll cross the stream, I have a

E♭   B♭   F7

dream, I'll cross the stream, I have a

B♭   F7

dream.

B♭ add sus   B♭   F7

B♭   B♭ add sus   B♭

dream,   I'll cross the stream,   I   have   a

dream, na na na na . . . . .

Repeat and fade out

40

The Winner Takes It All

Words & Music by Benny Andersson & Bjorn Ulvaeus.

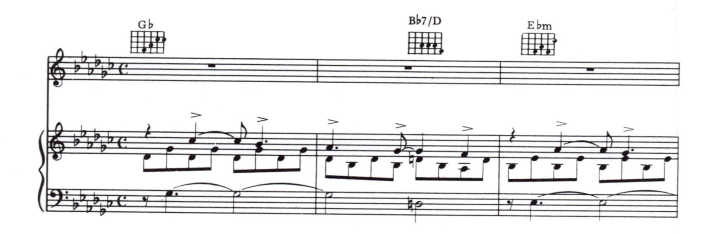

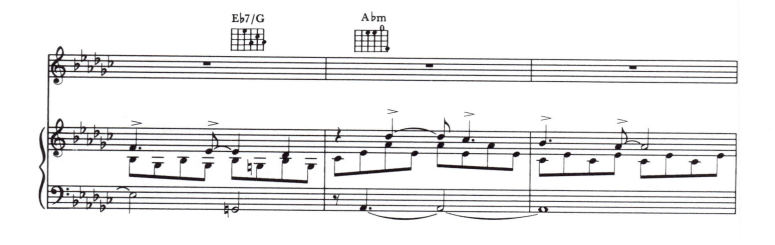

I don't wan - na

talk
arms
kiss
talk

a-bout things we've gone through,
think-ing I be-longed there,
like I used to kiss you,
if it makes you feel sad,

though it's hurt-ing
I fi-gured it made
does it feel the
and I un-der-

me,
sense,
same
stand

now it's his - to - ry.
build-ing me a fence,
when she calls your name.
you've come to shake my hand.

I've played all my
build-ing me a
Some-where deep in-
I a-po-lo-

cards
home,
-side
-gize

and that's what you've done too,
think - ing I'd be strong there,
you must know I miss you,
if it makes you feel bad

no-thing more to
but I was a
but what can I
see - ing me so

The win-ner takes it all,
The game is on a-gain,

the lo-ser has to
a lo-ver or a

fall,
friend,

it's sim-ple and it's plain,
a big thing or a small,

why should I com-plain.
the win-ner takes it all.

But tell me, does she

I don't wan-na

all.

The win - ner takes it

all.

Repeat and fade out

Money, Money, Money

Words & Music by Benny Andersson & Bjorn Ulvaeus.

work all night, I work all day to pay the bills I have to pay.___
man like that is hard to find, but I can't get him off my mind.___

Ain't it sad,_____ and
Ain't it sad,_____ and

S.O.S.

Words & Music by Benny Andersson, Bjorn Ulvaeus & Stig Anderson.

When you're gone, ___ how can I _____ ev - en try __ to go on? ___
When you're gone, ___ though I try, ___ how can I ___ car - ry on? ___

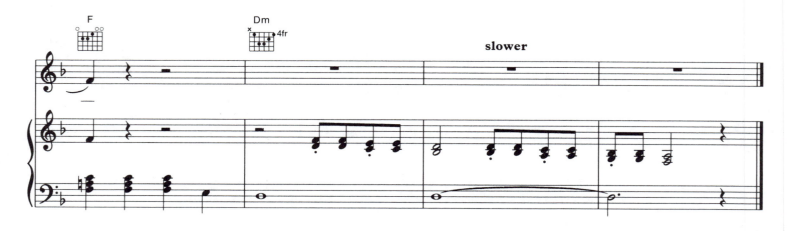

Chiquitita

Words & Music by Benny Andersson & Bjorn Ulvaeus.

for to-mor-row.
must re-ly on.
hard to hand-le.

How I hate to see you like this,
You were al-ways sure of your-self,
Chi-qui-ti-ta, tell me the truth,

there is no way you can de-ny it,
now I see you've bro-ken a feath-er,
there is no way you can de-ny it,

I can see that you're, oh, so
I hope we can patch it
I see that you're, oh, so

sad, so qui-et.
up to-geth-er.
sad, so qui-et.

Chi-qui-ti-ta, tell me the

Chi-qui-ti-ta, you and I

Fernando

Words & Music by Benny Andersson, Stig Anderson & Bjorn Ulvaeus.

my friend, Fer - nan - do.

slower

in tempo

D.𝄋 al Coda

⊕ CODA

There was some-thing in the

air that night, the stars___ were bright, Fer - nan - do.

They were shin-ing there for you and me,___ for lib - er - ty,___ Fer - nan -

- do. Though we ne - ver thought that we could lose,___ there's no re -

- gret. If I had to do the same a - gain___ I would

___ my friend, Fer - nan - do. If I had to do the

repeat and fade

Voulez Vous

Words & Music by Benny Andersson & Bjorn Ulvaeus.

1. Peo-ple ev-ery-where, a sense of ex-pec-ta-tion hang-in' in the air,
2. I know what you think — the girl means bus-iness so I'll of-fer her a drink —

vou - lez - vous.

Fm   D♭   B♭

C

to Coda

1. 2.

D.S. al

and here we

Fm

CODA

Vou - lez -

Fm

Fm   D♭

Repeat and fade out

Gimme! Gimme! Gimme!
(A Man After Midnight)

Words & Music by Benny Andersson & Bjorn Ulvaeus.

Half past twelve and I'm watch-in' the late show in my flat all a-lone, how I
Mo-vie stars find the end of the rain-bow with a for-tune to win, it's so

hate to spend the eve-ning on my own.
dif-ferent from the world I'm liv-in' in.
Au-tumn winds blow-in'
Tired of T - V I

out - side my win - dow as I look a - round the room, and it
o - pen the win - dow and I gaze in - to the night, but there's

makes me so de-pressed to see the gloom.
no - thing there to see, no - one in sight.

There's not a soul out there, _____ no - one to hear my prayer.

Gim-me! Gim-me! Gim-me! A man af - ter mid - night, won't some-bo - dy help me chase the

sha-dows a - way. Gim-me! Gim-me! Gim-me! A man af - ter mid - night, take

Does Your Mother Know

Words & Music by Benny Andersson & Bjorn Ulvaeus.

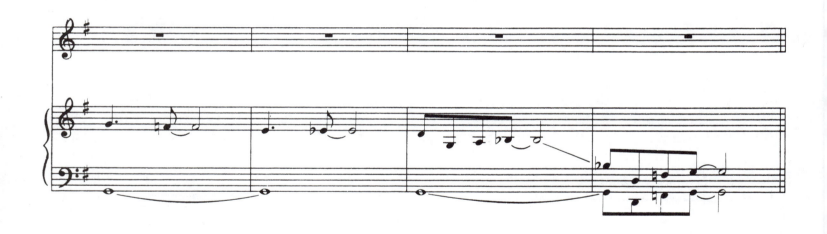

There's that look
You're so cute, I

in your eyes, I can read in your face that your feel-ings are driv-ing you wild,
like your style, and I know what you mean when you give me a flash of that smile,

ah, but girl, you're on-ly a child. ____
ah, but girl, you're on-ly a child. ____

CHORUS

Well, I could dance with you, ho-ney, if you think it's fun-ny, does

One Of Us

Words & Music by Benny Andersson & Bjorn Ulvaeus.

One of us is lone - ly, one of us__ is on - ly wait-ing for a call.

Sor - ry for her - self, feel-ing stu - pid, feeling small,

wish-ing she had nev-er left at all.__ Nev - er left at

all. Star-ing at the

D.S. and fade out

Thank You For The Music

Words & Music by Benny Andersson & Bjorn Ulvaeus.

The Name Of The Game

Words & Music by Benny Andersson, Stig Anderson & Bjorn Ulvaeus.

there's a lot you can teach___ me.___ So I wan-na know,
but it means a lot to___ me.___

what's the name of the game? Does it mean a-ny-thing___

___ to you?___ What's the name of the

game?___ Can you feel it the way___ I do?___

trust in you＿＿＿＿＿ would you let me down,＿＿＿＿＿ would you

laugh＿ at me?＿＿＿＿ If I said I care＿＿＿ for you,＿＿＿＿

could you feel the same＿＿＿ way too? I

wan - na know the name of the game.＿＿＿

Waterloo

Words & Music by Benny Andersson, Stig Anderson & Bjorn Ulvaeus.

-ter-loo, could-n't es-cape_ if I want - ed to. Wa-

-ter-loo, know-ing my fate_ is to be_____ with you. Wa,_

_ Wa Wa Wa Wa -ter-loo, fi - nal-ly fac - ing my Wa-

to Coda ⊕

1.

-ter-loo.   My, my_